GOOD DESIGN BOOKS ARE HARD TO FIND. IT TAKES YOU TIME AND MONEY TO GET THE RIGHT IMAGES & REFERENCES YOU NEED FOR YOUR WORK. BUT NOW YOU CAN HAVE IT ALL MORE EASILY. CHOOSE SIMPLY THE BEST IN ITS FIELD: BELVEDERE DESIGN-BOOKS, "MADE IN ITALY". GO, AND ASK FOR THE DESIGN-CLUB INTERNATIONAL AND YOU WILL GET A SPECIAL OFFER (FREE OF CHARGE) IMMEDIATELY. IT WILL SURPRISE YOU.

hit the point

È DIFFICILE TROVARE BUONI LIBRI DI DESIGN. CI VUOLE TEMPO E DENARO PER AVERE LE IMMAGINI E LE IDEE GIUSTE. MA ADESSO É TUTTO PIÚ FACILE. SCEGLIETE SOLAMENTE IL MEGLIO: I BELVEDERE-DESIGN-BOOKS, "MADE IN ITALY". CHIEDETE DEL DESIGN-CLUB INTERNATIONAL E AVRETE SUBITO GRATIS DELLE OFFERTE ECCEZIONALI CHE VI SORPRENDERANNO.

GUTE DESIGNBÜCHER SIND SCHWIERIG ZU FINDEN. ES ERFORDERT OFT VIEL ZEIT UND GELD, UM AN DIE RICHTIGEN IDEEN & VORLAGEN ZU GELANGEN. DOCH JETZT IST ALLES VIEL LEICHTER. WÄHLEN SIE EINFACH DAS BESTE: BELVEDERE-DESIGN-BOOKS, "MADE IN ITALY". ERKUNDINGEN SIE SICH NACH DEM DESIGN-CLUB INTERNATIONAL UND SIE WERDEN UNVERZÜGLICH & KOSTENLOS EIN SPEZIAL-ANGEBOT ERHALTEN, DAS SIE ÜBERRASCHEN WIRD.

ES REALMENTE DIFÍCIL ENCONTRAR BUENOS LIBROS DE DESIGN. SE NECESITAN TIEMPO Y DINERO PARA OBTENER LAS IMÁGENES & IDEAS APROPIADAS PARA VUESTRO TRABAJO. AHORA TODO ES MÁS FACIL. PUEDE CONSEGUIRSE LO MEJOR CON LOS BELVEDERE-DESIGN-BOOKS, "MADE IN ITALY". ES SUFICIENTE SOLICITARLOS AL DESIGN-CLUB INTERNATIONAL; INMEDIATAMENTE, Y GRATIS, RECIBIRÉIS MERAVILLOSAS OFERTAS.

IL N'EST PAS FACILE DE TROUVER DE BONS OUVRAGES DE DESIGN. VOUS AVEZ SANS DOUTE SOUVENT PERDU BEAUCOUP DE TEMPS ET D'ARGENT DANS LA RECHERCHE D'IMAGES & D'IDÉES NOUVELLES. AUJOURD'HUI CELA VOUS SERA PLUS FACILE. CHOISISSEZ TOUJOURS LE MEILLEUR: LES BELVEDERE-DESIGN-BOOKS, "MADE IN ITALY". ÉCRIVEZ AU DESIGN-CLUB INTERNATIONAL ET VOUS RECEVREZ GRATIS, ET PAR RETOUR DU CORRIER UNE OFFRE SPÉCIALE QUI VOUS SURPRENDRA AGRÉABLEMENT.

TAKE ALL THE ADVANTAGES OF THE DESIGN-CLUB!

APPROFITTA DEI VANTAGGI DEL DESIGN-CLUB!

NUTZEN SIE ALL DIE VORTEILE DES DESIGN-CLUB !

APROVECHEN DE LOS VANTAJAS DEL DESIGN-CLUB!

PROFITEZ DES AVANTAGES DU DESIGN-CLUB!

WRITE, CALL, OR FAX DIRECTLY AND WE WILL DO THE REST!

Desig

Basic series of Edition Belvedere: with extensive working material, ideas and informa
patterns with a wide variety of applications. Bound in hardcover or in a luxury paperback ve
All text are in five languages (English, Italian, German, Spanish and French). The large fo
(24 x 32 cm) is a standard like the international style of presentation. High quality pape
printing, mainly in full color. The series is constantly being extended with new themes and ti

GRAPHICOLOR
300 Graphic Motifs with
Fantasy in full color
ISBN 88-7070-033-X

BLACK AFRICA
Impressions: Graphic &
Color & Fashion & Design
ISBN 88-7070-022-4

DECOR
Illustrations of Wall-Deco-
rations - 1910-1920
ISBN 88-7070-004-6

ORIENTAL FLOWERS
Original Japanese Floral
Designs
ISBN 88-7070-005-7

ARCHITEXTURE
Historical Ornaments
& Architectural Designs
ISBN 88-7070-006-2

BOUQUETS
Floral Picture Postcards
from 1900-1950
ISBN 88-7070-008-9

FLORAL DREAM
Traditional Japanese Flower
Motifs - abstract, all in full color
ISBN 88-7070-007-0

MEMORY
Lace Designs and Textile
Decorations from ca. 1930
ISBN 88-7070-010-0

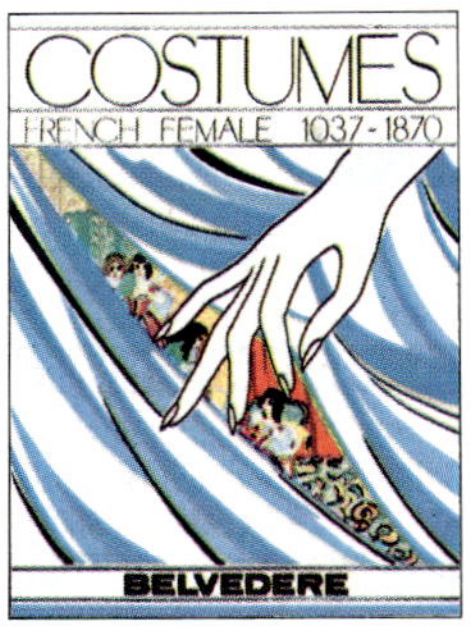

COSTUMES
French Female Costumes
(1037-1870)
ISBN 88-7070-009-7

SUITE No. 35
Decorative Art & Decorat
Fantasy fromthe 30th
ISBN 88-7070-011-9

FRESCO
Decorative & Graphic
& Fantasy Structures
ISBN 88-7070-012-7

PHOTO-FASHION
Photo / Graphic / Fashion
Images
ISBN 88-7070-013-5

ATLANTIS
Impressions from the Depth
of the Ocean
ISBN 88-7070-014-3

RHYTHMUSIC
Lines & Stripes in Variations
for Textile & Decoration
ISBN 88-7070-015-1

THE PLANTS OF 1917
125 Floral Plates in
Full Color
ISBN 88-7070-017-8

BLACK AFRICA
VOL. 1

BELVEDERE

BLACK AFRICA

VOL. 1

ARRANGED AND EDITED BY WOLFGANG HAGENEY

BELVEDERE
EDITION BELVEDERE CO. LTD., ROME - MILAN (ITALY)

BELVEDERE
DESIGNBOOK

FASHION TEXTILES GRAPHIC DESIGNS

VOLUME 2
PART I

BLACK AFRICA

IS PUBLISHED BY
EDITION BELVEDERE CO. LTD.
ROME-MILAN (ITALY)

PRINTED IN ITALY BY
STUDIO TIPOGRAFICO, ROME
PHOTOLITHOGRAPHY AND
COLOR SEPARATIONS BY
BELVEDERE LABORATORIES, ROME
LASER TYPE SETTING
COMP. LAB. BELVEDERE, ROME
LAYOUT & STYLING, ARTWORK
& GRAPHIC DESIGN BY
STUDIO BELVEDERE, ROME
ART DIRECTOR: HWH & BVR

PRINT PRODUCTION: MARCELLO CARMELLINI
STUDIO PRODUCTION: ROSA B. LENGSFELD
EDITOR & PUBLISHER: WOLFGANG H. HAGENEY

BELVEDERE PUBLICATIONS ARE AVAILABLE
THROUGH THE GENERAL BOOKTRADE,
ART SUPPLIES SHOPS, SPECIAL AGENTS OR
EXCLUSIVELY THROUGH THE INTERNATIONAL
BELVEDERE-DESIGN-CLUB BY WORLDWIDE
MAILORDER SYSTEM (FOR MEMBERS ONLY).

EDITION BELVEDERE CO. LTD.
00196 ROME / ITALY, PIAZZALE FLAMINIO, 19
TEL. (39-6) 320.44.88 - FAX (39-6) 320.29.60

ISBN 88-7070-023-2

Nature, light, color, lifestyle,
environment, clothing, jewellery ...
an ornamental, decorative, style of art ... a travel guide for the senses.

BLACK AFRICA

Africa is black ... negro & sun, heat & dust, steppe / savanna / desert & jungle, tropical creepers & liane, beasts of prey & wild cats, lions & leopards, snakes / crocodiles / tortoises / elephants, ostriches & zebras, mosquitoes & malaria, bushmen / medicinemen / tribal chiefs, rites & rituals, magic & superstition, gods & religions, masks & grimaces & dance & totem & rhythm & drumbeat, exorcism & ecstasy, rapture & torpidity, sacrifice & surrender, this life & the after-life, headdress & cannibalism, arrows / spears / lances, chains & pearls, bracelets & ivory, loincloths & tiger skin, kral & kisuaheli, clay huts & straw roofs & palm leaves...

Phantoms? Stereotypes? Nostalgic hocus-pocus? Or prejudice? The information which is daily transmitted to us through the mass-media and which should lay the foundations of our knowledge, springs from the treasure chest of African tomtom. Photo-safari, big-game hunt, tribal conflict, independence movements. They are scenes which arouse fascination, but are they true?

African theatre can indeed be staged with the help of these «props». In front of this scenery which stimulates and sets free the imagination, a picture of Africa develops — a picture full of suggestion. This image inspires the outsider so that he is tempted to endow it with new form. The patterns, models and clichées of our imaginative world clash with those of African reality which appear so strange to us. They conflict with the African culture that is so different from our own. An enrichment — perhaps even for both sides — arises out of this conflict.

The present day African contribution within international culture towards charging the conventional image of the «black continent» is very modest and scarcely acknowledged. Africa possesses no convincing selfportrait in which the cult and culture of the past is confronted with that of the present, for example, through the medium of art. One remains complacently content with the familiar. The sight of sculptures and masks, jewellery and weapons, wildcat furs and elephant tusks, wooden carvings and other such phenomena, is, on the one hand, attractive but on the other hand, has become reduced to a lifeless ritual. It creates the impression that African art lies dormant; well-preserved within a sarcophagus.

And yet Afro-culture is vitally alive. And hasn't modern art profitted from this fact up until now? Isn't African culture a fascinating mine of resources just as much now in the present as it has been in the past? Africa, with its «primitive art» still possesses an immeasurable potential: originality, spontaneity, instinct, imagination and self-confidence — characteristics of the inner and outer structure of this continent.

This book shows African folklore transformed into graphic design, where nature, light, color, lifestyle, environment, clothing and jewellery are symbolically represented. The result is a free graphic interpretation of the African form of expression and creation. An ornamental/decorative style of art — a travel guide for the senses. The journey leads through a stream of archaic fantasies. A wide spectrum of colors, shapes, patterns and compositions is opened up whereby the suggested solutions are in no way to be understood as the last link in the chain of imaginative thought.

AFRICA NERA

L'Africa è nera ... negri & sole, calura & polvere, steppa / savana / regione selvaggia & giungla, piante sarmentose & liane, belve feroci & felini, leoni & leopardi, serpenti / coccodrilli / tartarughe / elefanti, struzzi & zebre, zanzare & malaria, boscimani / stregoni / capi tribú, riti & rituali, magia & superstizione, dei & religioni, maschere & smorfie & totem & ritmo & rullo di tamburi, scongiuri & estasi, contemplazione & paralisi, sacrificio & abnegazione, vita terrena & trascendenza, ornamenti del capo & cannibalismo, freccie / giavellotti / lancie, collane & perle, bracciali & avorio, perizoma & pelli di tigre, kraal & kisuaheli, capanne d'argilla & tetti di paglia & foglie di palme ...

Immagini fantasma? Stereotipi? Abracadabra nostalgico? O soltanto malintesi? Le informazioni che ogni giorno ci vengono trasmesse (attraverso i massmedia) e che dovrebbero consolidare la nostra conoscenza derivano dalla cassa di cianfrusaglie del tam tam africano. Fotosafari, caccia grossa, lotte tribali, movimenti di indipendenza. Frasi fatte affascinanti. Sono giusti i requisiti? Il teatro africano si può certamente mettere in scena con tutto questo. Di fronte a questa scena che comunica sí numerosi stimoli e libera la fantasia emerge un'immagine di Africa piena di suggestioni.

Numerose ispirazioni si rivelano ad un osservatore esterno che cerca di dare loro una nuova forma.

Modelli, schemi, cliché che emergono dalla nostra immaginazione contrastano con la realtà africana per noi cosí estranea — con una cultura africana cosí diversa dalla nostra.

Da questo contrasto deriva talvolta un arricchimento — forse persino per entrambe.

Il contributo che oggi gli africani portano allo sviluppo culturale internazionale per trasformare l'immagine stereotipa del «continente nero» ha un effetto modesto e poca risonanza.

Manca ancora un'autorappresentazione convincente dell'Africa in cui il confronto del culto e della cultura del passato con il presente venga diffuso con mezzi artistici. Ci si accontenta ancora sempre di ciò che è conosciuto.

La vista di sculture e maschere, ornamenti e armi, belve e zanne d'elefante, legno intagli e simili da una parte attrae, dall'altra è come un rigido rito. Se ne ricava l'impressione di una tranquilla arte africana ben protetta in un sarcofago. Ma la cultura africana è anche vitalità massima.

Non ne ha forse approfittato fino ad oggi la cultura moderna? Non è forse la cultura africana oggi come sempre un serbatoio affascinante?

L'Africa con la sua «arte primitiva» dispone sempre di un potenziale incommensurabile: originalità, spontaneità, istinto, fantasia e insieme fiducia in se stessi; caratteristiche queste di una struttura culturale interna ed esterna propria di questo continente.

Questo libro presenta il folklore africano tradotto in design grafico, per cui natura, luce, colori, modi di vivere, ambiente, costume e ornamenti sono resi nella pienezza del loro significato simbolico. Ne risulta una interpretazione grafica-libera delle forme espressive e creative africane.

Una stilistica ornativo/decorativa, una guida dei sensi — un viaggio attraverso un fiume di fantasie arcaiche.

Vi si rivela come in un caleidoscopio un ampio spettro di colori, forme, figure e composizione, ma le soluzioni offerte in nessun caso devono essere intese come ultima possibilità di una lunga serie di pensieri e di fantasia.

SCHWARZAFRIKA

Afrika ist schwarz ... Neger & Sonne, Hitze & Staub, Steppe / Savanna / Wildnis & Dschungel, Schlingpflanzen & Lianen, Raubtiere & Wildkatzen, Löwen & Leoparden, Schlangen / Krokodile / Schildkröten / Elefanten, Strauße & Zebras, Moskitos & Malaria, Buschmänner / Medizinmänner / Stammesfürsten, Riten & Rituale, Magie & Aberglaube, Götter & Religionen, Masken & Fratzen & Tanz & Totem & Rhythmus & Trommelschlag, Beschwörung & Verzückung, Ekstase & Erstarrung, Opfer & Hingabe, Diesseits & Jenseits, Kopfschmuck & Kannibalismus, Pfeile / Speere / Lanzen, Ketten & Perlen, Armreifen & Elfenbein, Lendenschurz & Tigerfelle, Kral & Kisuaheli, Lehmhütten & Strohdächer & Palmblätter ...

Phantombilder? Stereotypen? Nostalgischer Hokuspokus? Oder lauter Mißverständnisse? Die Informationen, die uns täglich (durch die Massenmedien) vermittelt werden und unseren Wissensstand untermauern sollen, entstammen durchaus der Plunderkiste des afrikanischen Tamtam. Fotosafari, Großwildjagd, Stammesfehden, Unabhängigkeitsbewegungen. Gemeinplätze, die auch Faszination auslösen. Doch stimmen die Requisiten? Afrikanisches Theater läßt sich bestimmt damit inszenieren. Vor dieser Kulisse, die so viel Anregung vermittelt und Phantasie freisetzt, entsteht folglich ein Afrikabild voller suggestiver Ausstrahlung. Es offenbahrt sich dem Außenstehenden eine Vielfalt an Inspirationen, wobei man versucht ist, ihr eine neue Gestalt zu geben. Es reiben sich die Muster, Raster und Klischees aus unserer Vorstellungswelt mit denen der afrikanischen Wirklichkeit, die uns so fremd scheint — mit der afrikanischen Kultur, die der unserigen so konträr ist. Aus dieser Reibung entsteht zuweilen eine Bereicherung — vielleicht sogar für beide Seiten.

Der Beitrag, den die Afrikaner heute zum internationalen Kulturgeschehen leisten, um das nun einmal geprägte Bild vom «schwarzen Erdteil» zu verändern, wirkt bescheiden und findet kaum Resonanz. Eine überzeugende Selbstdarstellung Afrikas in der die Konfrontation von Kult und Kultur der Vergangenheit mit der Gegenwart etwa mit den Mitteln der Kunst ausgetragen wird, steht noch aus. Noch immer begnügt man sich mit Vertrautem. Der Anblick von Skulpturen und Masken, Schmuck und Waffen, Raubtierfellen und Elefantenzähnen, Holzschnitzereien und dergleichen mehr ist einerseits reizvoll, anderseits aber auch schon zum Ritual erstarrt. Der Eindruck entsteht, als ruhe afrikanische Kunst wohlbehütet in einem Sarkophag. Dabei ist die Afro-Kultur von höchster Lebendigkeit. Hat nicht die moderne Kunst bis in die Gegenwart hinein davon profitiert? Ist die afrikanische Kultur nicht nach wie vor ein faszinierendes Reservoir?

Noch immer verfügt Afrika mit seiner «Primitivkunst» über ein unermeßliches Potential: Ursprünglichkeit, Spontaneität, Instinkt, Phantasie oder auch Selbstvertrauen. Kennzeichen für das innere und äußere Gefüge dieses Kontinents.

Das vorliegende Buch zeigt afrikanische Folklore, umgesetzt in graphisches Design, wobei Natur, Licht, Farben, Lebensweise, Umwelt, Kleidung oder Schmuck sinnbildhaft dargestellt sind. Entstanden ist eine freie, graphische Interpretation afrikanischer Ausdrucks- und Gestaltungsformen. Eine ornamentale / dekorative Stilkunde — ein Reiseführer für die Sinne. Die Fahrt führt über einen Strom archaischer Phantasien. Es eröffnet sich kaleidoscopartig ein breites Spektrum aus Farben, Formen, Figurationen und Kompositionen, wobei die angebotenen Lösungen keinesfalls als letztes Glied einer langen Gedanken- und Phantasiekette zu verstehen sind.

AFRICA NEGRA

Africa es negra ... negros & sol, calor & polvo, estepa / sabana / desierto & jungla, plantas trepadoras & lianas, fieras & felinos, leones & leopardos, serpientes / cocodrilos / tortugas / elefantes, avestruces & cebras, mosquitos & malaria, bosquimanes / hechiceros / caciques, ritos & rituales, magia & superstición, dioses & religiones, máscaras & muecas & danza & totems & ritmo & batir de tambores, conjuración & arrobamiento, éxtasis & estremecimiento, sacrificio & entrega, mundo terrenal & más allá, adornos de cabeza & canibalismo, flechas / jabalinas / lanzas, collares & perlas, pulseras & marfil, pequeños mandiles & pieles de tigre, kral & kisuaeli, cabañas de barro & techos de paja & hojas de palmera ...

Imágenes fántasma? Ideas estereotipadas? Ilusión nostálgica? O una serie de malentendidos? Las informaciones que nos llegan diariamente a través de los medios de comunicación social y que deberían apuntalar nuestro nivel de conocimientos proceden muchas veces de creencias basadas como trastos viejos en el tam-tam africano. Fotosafaris, caza mayor, enfrentamientos entre tribus, movimientos independentistas. Lugares comunes que desencadenan también una cierta fascinación. Pero son estos los requisitos adecuados. El teatro se podría ciertamente escenificar con tales medios. Ante este trasfondo, que proporciona tantas sugerencias y deja libre la fantasía, surge una imagen de Africa llena de sugestiva irradiación. Para el que lo contempla se abre una amplia panorámica de inspiraciones y siente a la vez la tentación de darles una nueva forma.

Las muestras, baremos y clichés del mundo de nuestra imaginacion tropiezan con las de la realidad africana, tan extraña para nosotros, así como con las de la cultura africana tan contraria a la nuestra. De esta fricción se obtiene a veces un enriquecimiento, incluso para ambas partes. La aportación actual de los africanos al acontecer cultural internacional, de cara a modificar la imagen tan fuertemente acuñada del llamado «Continente Negro», puede parecer modesta y apenas encuentra resonancia.

Falta aún, por ejemplo, una convincente autorrepresentación de Africa en la que la confrontación de culto y cultura, del pasado y el presente, se dilucide por ejemplo por medios artistícos. En general continuamos conformándonos con cosas conocidas. La imagen de esculturas y máscaras, adornos y armas, pieles de animales carniceros y colmillos de elefante, tallas en madera y obras similares, tiene sin duda gran encanto pero, por otra parte, se ha petrificado hasta convertirse en un ritual. Surge la impresión de que el arte africano descansa cobijado en una especie de sarcófago.

Sin embargo, la afrocultura goza de la mayor vitalidad. Es que el arte moderno, hasta el presente, no se ha beneficiado de esta circunstancia? Es que no sigue siendo la cultura africana una reserva fascinante? Africa, con su «arte primitivo», continúa teniendo un potencial inmenso: naturalidad, espontaneidad, instinto, fantasía y también confianza en si misma; características de la estructura interior y exterior de este continente.

El presente libro muestra folclore africano transformado en diseño gráfico, en el que la naturaleza, la luz, los colores, la forma de vida, el medio ambiente, el atuendo o los adornos, están representados simbólicamente. Ha surgido una interpretación gráfica libre de formas de expresión africanas. Se trata de una estilística ornamental/decorativa, una guía para los sentidos. El viaje lleva a un gran rio de fantásias arcaicar. A manera de caleidoscopio, se nos abre un amplio espectro de colores, formas, figuras y composiciones, en las que las soluciones ofrecidas no deben ser interpretadas como un último eslabón de una larga cadena de ideas y de fantasía.

AFRIQUE NOIR

L'Afrique est noire ... nègre & soleil, chaleur & poussière, steppe / savane / désert & jungle, plantes grimpantes & lianes, fauves & félidés, lions & léopards, serpents / crocodiles / tortues / éléphants, autruches & zèbres, moustiques & malaria, sauvages / sorciers / chefs de tribus, rites & rituels, magie & superstition, dieux & religions, masques & grimaces & danse & totems & rythmes & tam-tam, invocation & extase, contemplation & paralysie, sacrifices & abnégation, ici & là, parure de tête & cannibalisme, flèches / javelots / lances, chaînes & perles, bracelets & ivoire, pagne & peau de tigre, kraal & kisuaheli, cabane en torchis & toits de paille & feuilles de palmiers...

Des portraits-robots? des stéréotypes? de nostalgiques visions? ou bien une foule de malentendus? Les informations que nous recevons chaque jour (par les médias) et qui doivent améliorer notre niveau de connaissances, viennent tout droit d'un fatras inspiré du tam-tam africain. Safaris-photo, chasse aux fauves, hainestribales, mouvements d'indépèndance. Ce sont des lieux communs qui exercent cependant une certaine fascination. Qu'y-a-t-il de vrai là-dedans? On peut certes en tirer du théâtre africain. Devant un tel décor qui stimule l'imagination, se forme une image très suggestive de l'Afrique. Une multitude d'impressions s'offre à l'observateur non averti, impressions auxquelles on s'efforce de trouver une forme nouvelle. Les motifs, trames et chichés de notre monde imaginaire et ceux de la réalité africaine qui nous est si étrangère, de la culture africaine si différente de la nôtre, se trouvent confrontés. De cette confrontation naît parfois un enrichissement — peut-être même pour les deux parties. Ce que les Africains apportent aujourd'hui au développement culturel international, afin de modifier cette image consacrée du «continent noir», paraît relativement modeste et trouve bien peu d'écho. Il n'existe pas encore de présentation convaincante de l'Afrique par elle-même, de cette Afrique dans laquelle l'affrontement des cultes et de la culture du passé avec le présent se manifeste au moyen de l'art. On se satisfait encore de ce qui est familier. La contemplation de sculptures et de masques, de bijoux et d'armes, de peaux de bêtes et de défenses d'éléphants, de sculptures sur bois et autres a certainement son charme, mais d'un autre côté, elle fait déjà partie d'un rituel. On a l'impression que l'art africain repose bien à l'abri dans un sarcophage. Pourtant, la culture africaine est pleine de vitalité. L'art moderne n'en a-t-il pas profité jusque de nos jours encore? La culture africaine ne reste-t-elle pas un fascinant réservoir? L'Afrique dispose toujours, grâce à son «art primitif», d'un potentiel sans mesure: originalité, spontanéité, instinct, imagination, mais aussi confiance en soi—telles sont les caractéristiques de la structure intérieure et extérieure de ce continent.

Le présent ouvrage propose du folklore africain transformé en dessin graphique, la nature, la lumière, les couleurs, le mode de vie, l'environnement, l'habillement ou les bijoux y étant représentés sous une forme symbolique. Il en résulte une interprétation graphique, libre, des formes d'expression africaines. Une leçon de style ornemental/décoratif — un guide des sens. Le voyage se déroule sur le courant de visions archaïques. C'est un spectre étendu de couleurs, de formes, de figures et de compositions qui se déploie comme un kaléidoscope, les solutions proposées n'étant en aucun cas à considérer comme les dernier maillon d'une longue chaîne de pensées et de visions.

The designs of this volume were created and developed in the studio & laboratory of the Edition Belvedere in Rome/Italy under the general direction and editor-ship of Wolfgang Hageney.
Following members belonged to the design team —
Diana Lelli / Luce Delhove
Antonello Martino / Luigi Deleo
Francesca Schiavon / Anna Maria Troiani / Etsuko Kakui

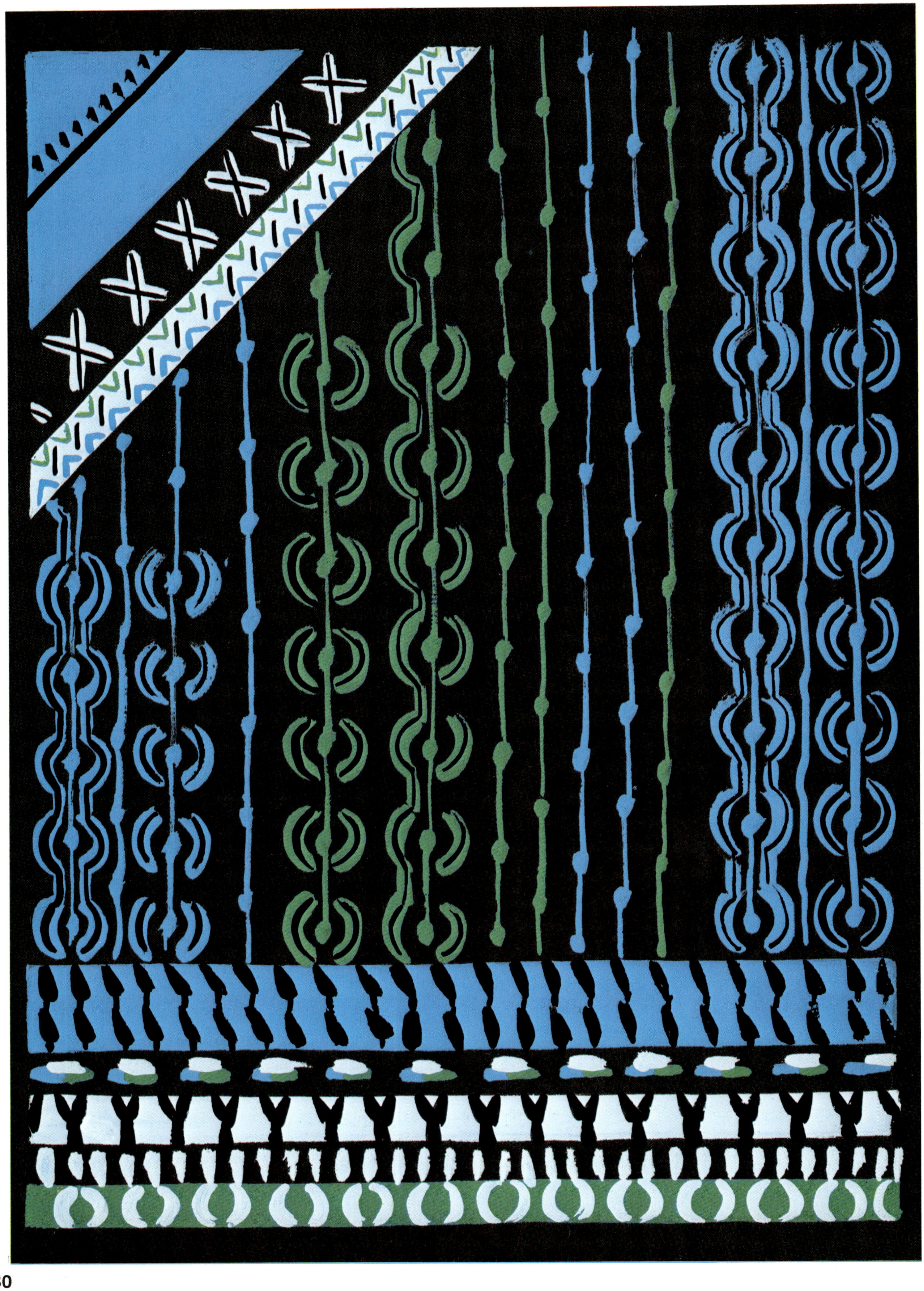

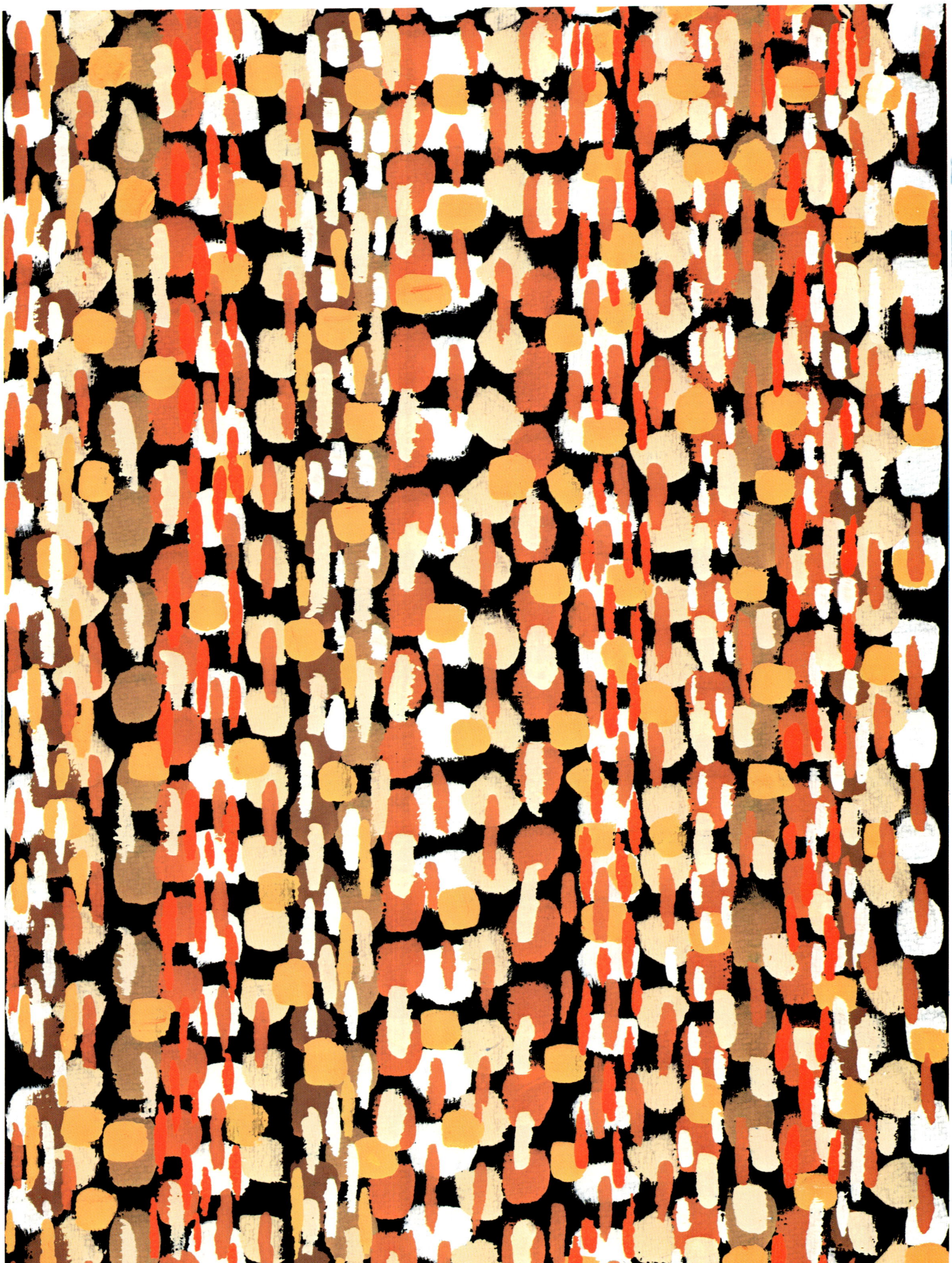

ADVERTISING
GRAPHIC DESIGN
CERAMICS
INTERIOR DESIGN
ARCHITECTURE
TEXTILE / FABRICS
DECORATION
LAYOUT / STYLING
DESIGN
PASSPORT
TYPOGRAPHY
FASHION / MODE
CLIP-ART
COMPUTER GRAPHIC
EDITION BELVEDERE CO. LTD. 00196 ROME/ITALY, PIAZZALE FLAMINIO 19. TEL. (06) 320.44.88
BELVEDERE
EDITION BELVEDERE CO. LTD.
PIAZZALE FLAMINIO, 19
00196 ROME/ITALY

Books

Collana principale della Edition Belvedere, ideata per i professionisti: ricca fonte di materiale per il lavoro, di idee ed informazioni, di motivi con ampie possibilitá di applicazione. I libri sono rilegati a filo refe o con legatura a brossura. I testi sono in cinque lingue (inglese, italiano, tedesco, spagnolo, francese). I volumi, tutti di grande formato (24 x 32 cm) sono creati per una diffusione internazionale. La carta e la stampa a colori sono di alta qualitá. La serie si accresce sempre di nuovi argomenti.

Basis-Reihe der Edition Belvedere, speziell für Professionelle, kulturell Interessierte sowie Kollektionisten und Anwendern von grafisch-visuellen Design-Dokumenten. D.h.: umfangreiches Arbeitsmaterial, ständig neue Ideen und detaillierte Informationen sowie Vorlagen mit vielseitigen Anwendungsmöglichkeiten. Sämtliche Texte in fünf Sprachen (englisch, italienisch, deutsch, spanisch, französisch). Großformatige, internationale Aufmachung (24 x 32 cm). Gebunden im Hardcover oder in der großen Paperback-Version. Qualitativ hochwertiger Druck, meist in voller Farbe, auf Kunstdruck-Papier. Diese Reihe wird ständig mit neuen Themen fortgesetzt.

GRAPHIC FLOWER
From Dresses & Fabrics between 1930-1950
ISBN 88-7070-025-9

DECORATIVE ORNAMENT
Floral/Graphical/Ornamental/ Figurative
ISBN 88-7070-028-3

REPERTOIRE
Modern Interior Design 1928 - 1929
ISBN 88-7070-068-2

PARIS 1928 - 1929
Graphic Collection of Designs & Visual Art
ISBN 88-7070-069-0

THE PICTORIAL HAND - BOOK OF CREATIVE GRAPHIC DESIGN
ISBN 88-7070-072-0

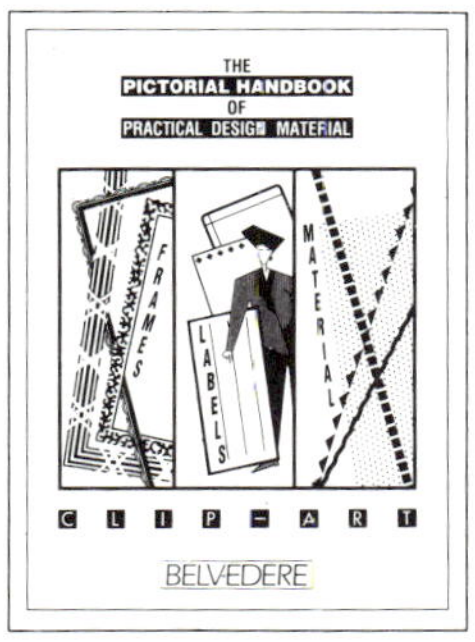

THE PICTORIAL HAND - BOOK OF PRACTICAL DESIGN MATERIAL
ISBN 88-7070-073-9

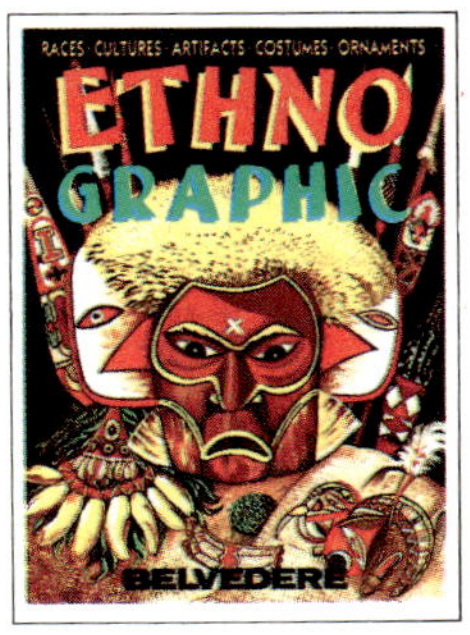

ETHNO-GRAPHIC
Races & Cult & Articraft Costume & Ornaments
ISBN 88-7070-074-7

JAPAN IDEABOOK
Kimono-Designs, Graphic & Floreal & Geom.
ISBN 88-7070-075-5

TEXTILE PATTERNBOOK
Floral - Graphic & Geometric Designs
ISBN 88-7070-076-3

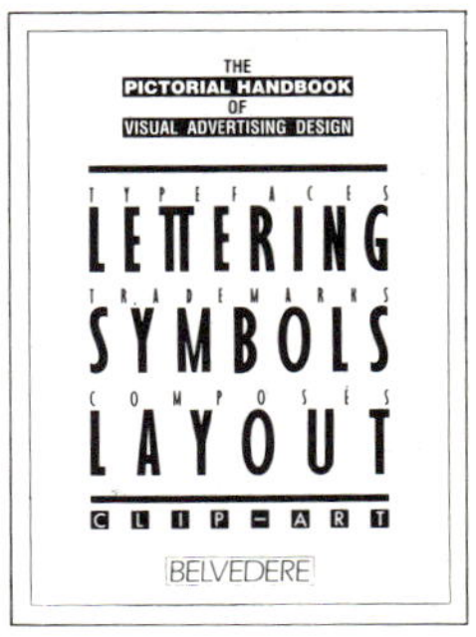

THE PICTORIAL HAND - BOOK OF VISUAL ADVERTISING DESIGN
ISBN 88-7070-077-1

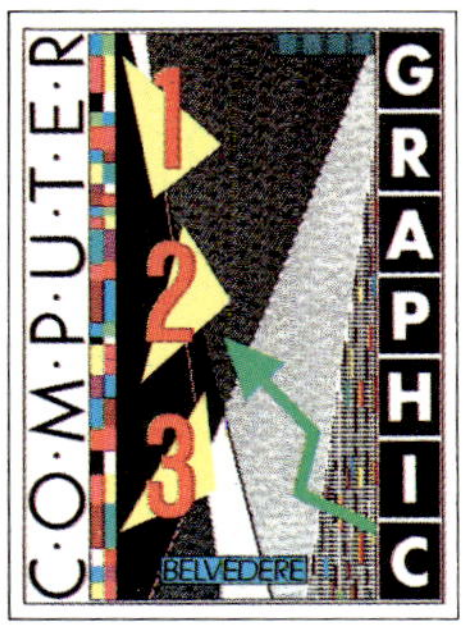

COMPUTER GRAPHIC II
Creative Graphic Design on Personal Computers
ISBN 88-7070-102-6

GRAFIX I (Fantasy)
Clip-Art,Layout,Desktop Publ., Graphic Design
ISBN 88-7070-104-2

FLORAL ART
Flower Arrangements & Decor & Modern Style
ISBN 88-7070-079-8

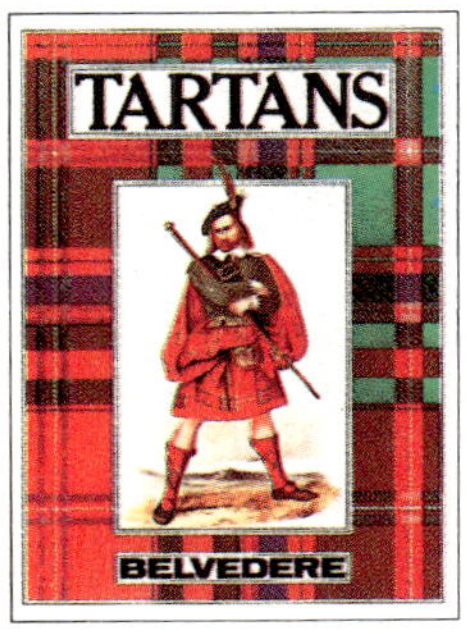

TARTANS
Tartans of Clans & Septs with Arms of Chiefs
ISBN 88-7070-080-1

COLOR SYMPHONY
Dark & Light Graphic designs, Floral Graphic & Floral designs,
ISBN 88-7070-132-8

Design-Books

GRAPHICOLOR - Vol. 1
150 single Graphic Motifs full of Fantasy
ISBN 88-7070-034-8

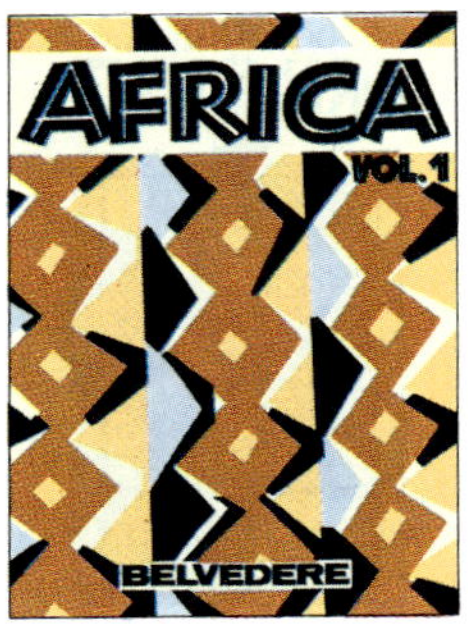

AFRICA - Vol. 1
Impressions: Graphic & Color & Fashion
ISBN 88-7070-023-2

FRESCO - Vol. 1
Decorative & Graphic Fantasy Structures
ISBN 88-7070-020-8

GRAPHIC FLOWER - Vol. 1
Graphic Designs & Motifs from Dress Fabrics (1930-1950)
ISBN 88-7070-026-7

PARIS - Vol. 1 (1928)
Collection of Design & Visual Art - 1928
ISBN 88-7070-092-5

GRAPHICOLOR - Vol. 2
150 single Graphic Motifs full of Fantasy
ISBN 88-7070-035-6

AFRICA - Vol. 2
Impressions: Graphic & Color & Fashion
ISBN 88-7070-024-0

FRESCO - Vol. 2
Decorative & Graphic Fantasy Structures
ISBN 88-7070-021-6

GRAPHIC FLOWER - Vol. 2
Graphic Designs & Motifs from Dress Fabrics (1930-1950)
ISBN 88-7070-027-5

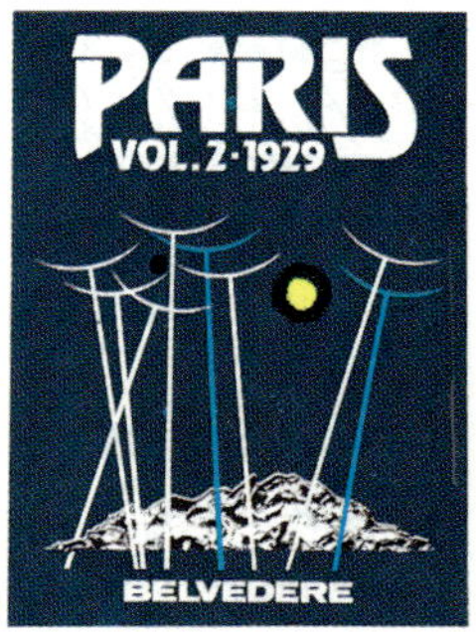

PARIS - Vol. 2 (1929)
Collection of Design & Visual Art - 1929
ISBN 88-7070-093-3

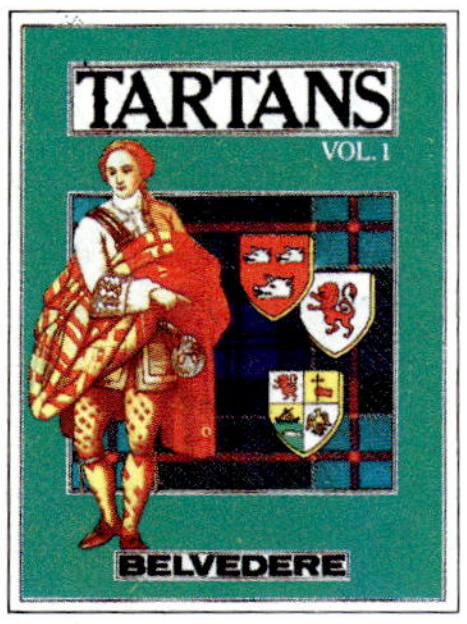

TARTANS - Vol. 1
Tartans of Clans & Septs with Arms of Chiefs
ISBN 88-7070-081-X

DECORATIVE ORNAMENT
Vol. 1 Graphic Motifs - all in full color
ISBN 88-7070-029-1

DECORATIVE ORNAMENT
Vol. 3 Ornamental Motifs - all in full color
ISBN 88-7070-031-3

COLOR LEGEND - Vol. 1
Free-hand creative motifs
Dark Graphic Designs
ISBN 88-7070-145-X

COLOR LEGEND - Vol. 3
Free-hand creative motifs
Floral Graphic Designs
ISBN 88-7070-147-6

TARTANS - Vol. 2
Tartans of Clans & Septs with Arms of Chiefs
ISBN 88-7070-082-8

DECORATIVE ORNAMENT
Vol. 2 Floral Motifs - all in full color
ISBN 88-7070-030-5

DECORATIVE ORNAMENT
Vol 4 Figurative Motifs - mostly in full color
ISBN 88-7070-032-1

COLOR LEGEND - Vol. 2
Free-hand creative motifs
Light Graphic Designs
ISBN 88-7070-146-8

COLOR LEGEND - Vol. 4
Free-hand creative motifs
Floral Designs
ISBN 88-7070-148-4

Paperbacks

THE PLANTS - Vol. 1
Floral Plates - (Spring I)
ISBN 88-7070-087-9

THE PLANTS - Vol. 2
Floral Plates - (Spring II)
ISBN 88-7070-088-7

THE PLANTS - Vol. 3
Floral Plates - (Summer I)
ISBN 88-7070-089-5

THE PLANTS - Vol. 4
Floral Plates - (Summer II)
ISBN 88-7070-090-9

THE PLANTS - Vol. 5
Floral Plates -
(Fall & Winter)
ISBN 88-7070-091-7

TEXTILE PATTERNBOOK, Vol.1
Graphic Monotone
Patterns & Designs
ISBN 88-7070-142-5

FLORAL ART - Vol. 1
Flower Arrangements
& Decor & Modern Style
ISBN 88-7070-124-7

COMPUTER GRAPHIC II, Vol.1
Creative Graphic Design
on Personal Computers
ISBN 88-7070-118-2

REPERTOIRE - Vol. 1
Modern Interior Design
1928-1929
ISBN 88-7070-096-8

REPERTOIRE - Vol. 5
Modern Interior Design
1928-1929
ISBN 88-7070-100-X

TEXTILE PATTERNBOOK, Vol.2
Floral Monotone
Patterns & Designs
ISBN 88-7070-143-3

FLORAL ART - Vol. 2
Flower Arrangements
& Decor & Modern Style
ISBN 88-7070-125-5

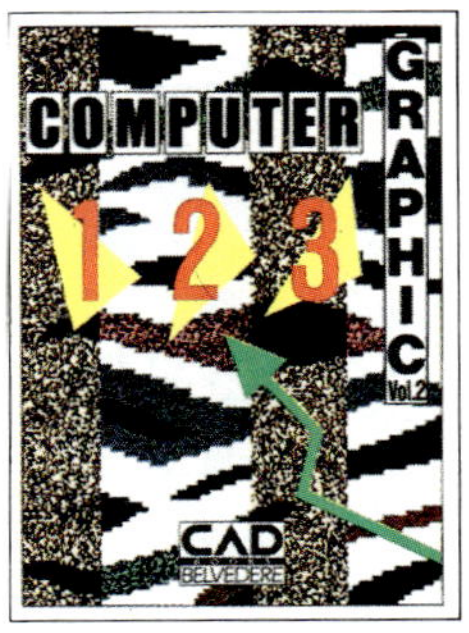

COMPUTER GRAPHIC II, Vol.2
Creative Graphic Design
on Personal Computers
ISBN 88-7070-119-0

ETHNO-GRAPHIC - Vol. 1
Race & Cult & Articraft
Costume & Ornaments
ISBN 88-7070-083-6

ETHNO-GRAPHIC - Vol. 3
Races & Cult & Articraft
Costume & Ornaments
ISBN 88-7070-085-2

TEXTILE PATTERNBOOK, Vol.3
Geometric Monotone
Patterns & Designs
ISBN 88-7070-144-1

FLORAL ART - Vol. 3
Flower Arrangements
& Decor & Modern Style
ISBN 88-7070-126-3

COMPUTER GRAPHIC II, Vol.3
Creative Graphic Design
on Personal Computers
ISBN 88-7070-120-4

ETHNO-GRAPHIC - Vol. 2
Races & Cult & Articraft
Costume & Ornaments
ISBN 88-7070-084-4

ETHNO-GRAPHIC - Vol. 4
Races & Cult & Articraft
Costume & Ornaments
ISBN 88-7070-086-0

Designer's - Notebooks

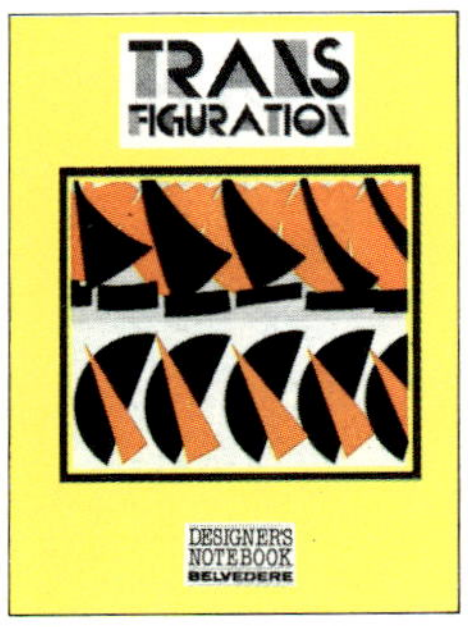

TRANSFIGURATION
Decorative Graphic 1930
Japan/Europa
ISBN 88-7070-036-4

FLOREAL
Decorative Flower Motifs
Modern Style
ISBN 88-7070-037-2

CHINESE CERAMICS
Decorative Motifs from
Chinese Pottery
ISBN 88-7070-038-0

JAPAN PATTERNS
500 Motifs from Original
Kimono Designs
ISBN 88-7070-039-9

MIRACLE
Costumes - Lace
Theatre - Poetry
ISBN 88-7070-040-2

NATURAL FLOWERS
Basic Motifs of Natural
Flowers & Herbs
ISBN 88-7070-041-0

MODE 1924
Fashion Designs &
Decorative Illustrations
ISBN 88-7070-042-9

FOLK
Textiles / Native Designs /
Ornaments
ISBN 88-7070-043-7

MODE 1938
Fashion Designs /
Decorative Illustrations
ISBN 88-7070-044-5

DECO - IDEAS
Floral & Graphic & Figurative
Art-Deco-Designs
ISBN 88-7070-045-3

LACE - VIENNA
Lace & Embroidery Patterns
Liberty Style
ISBN 88-7070-052-6

GERMAN JEWELLERY
Variations of Jewellery Designs
Liberty Style
ISBN 88-7070-053-4

MELANCHOLY
Floral Motifs & Designs
Liberty Style
ISBN 88-7070-054-2

JAPAN MOTIFS
Designs from Japanese
Kimono Motifs
ISBN 88-7070-055-0

KIMONO
Japan Designs & Flowers
& Animals & Nature
ISBN 88-7070-057-7

KASHMIR
Classical & Basic cashmere &
paisley motifs - monotone style
ISBN 88-7070-059-3

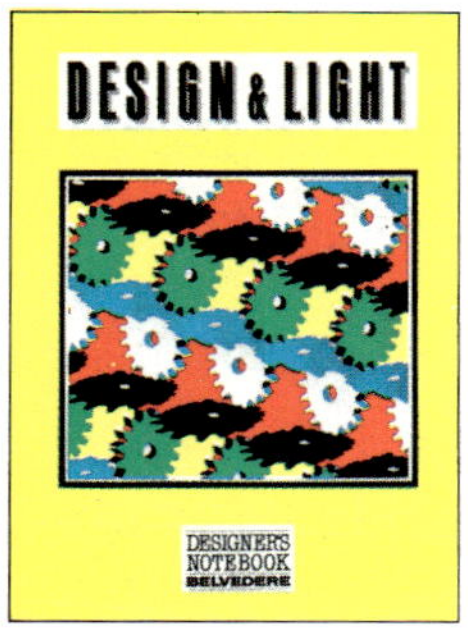

DESIGN & LIGHT
3-D Color Effects +
Abstract Des. Patterns
ISBN 88-7070-063-1

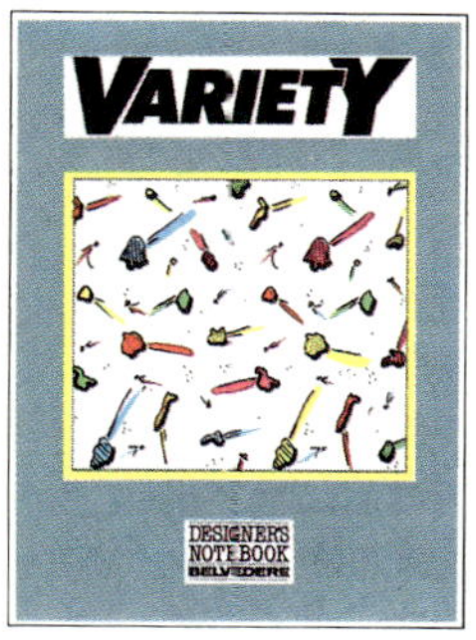

VARIETY
Modern Monotones From
the Sign to the Design
ISBN 88-7070-064-X

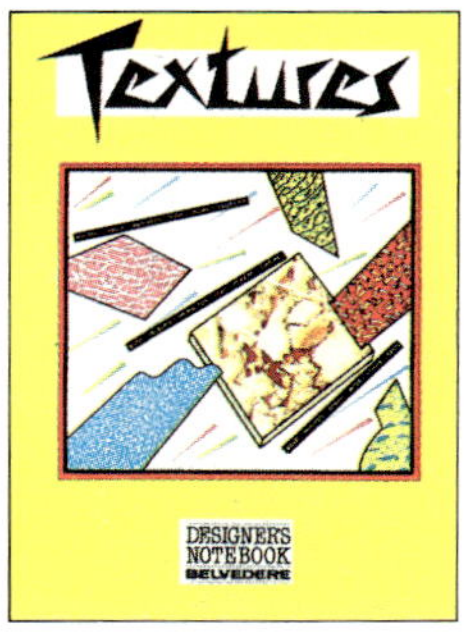

TEXTURES
Basic Nature Motifs
Ground Designs
ISBN 88-7070-065-8

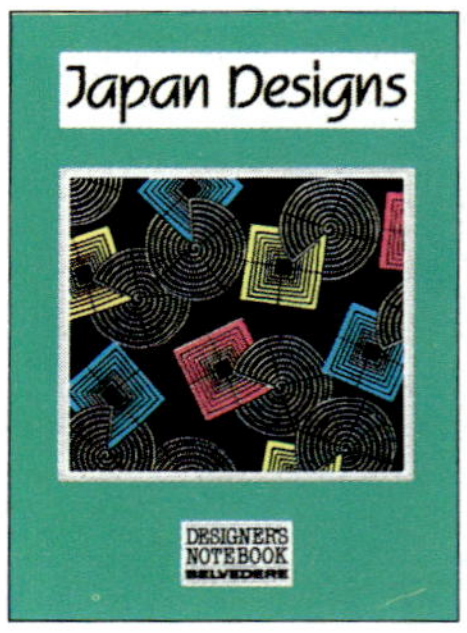

JAPAN DESIGNS
Designs from Japanese
Kimono Motifs
ISBN 88-7070-078-X

Clip - Art - Books

REF.-BOOK 1
Copyright-free Images of Figures - Vehicles - Buildings - Landscapes
ISBN 88-7070-046-1

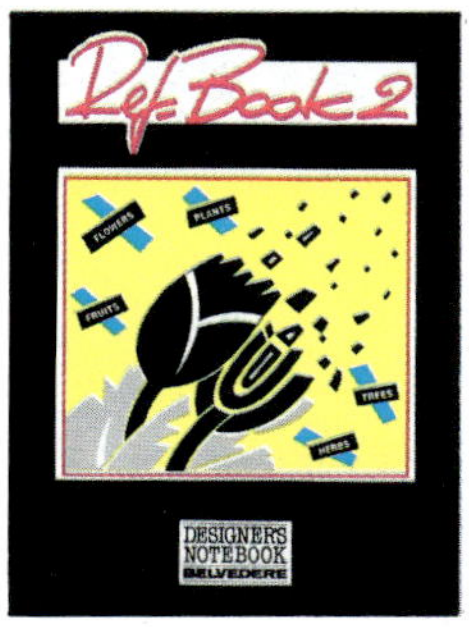

REF.-BOOK 2
Copyright-free Images of Flowers - Fruits - Trees - Plants - Herbs
ISBN 88-7070-047-X

REF.-BOOK 3
Copyright-free Images of Animals - Birds, Insects, Fishes, Wild Animals
ISBN 88-7070-048-8

REF.-BOOK 4
Copyright-free Images of Historic Theatre Wardrobe
ISBN 88-7070-049-6

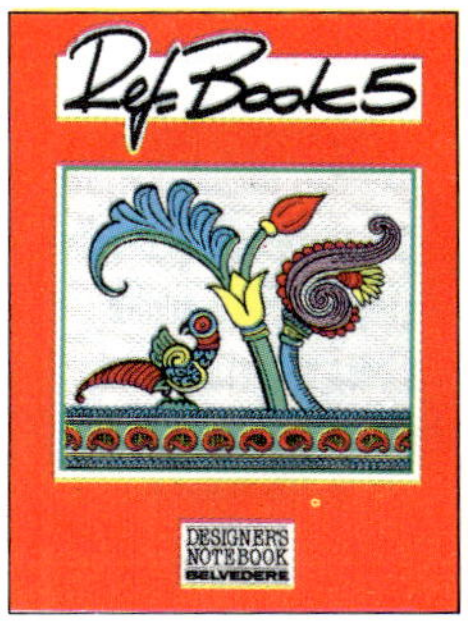

REF.-BOOK 5
Copyright-free Images of Historical & Modern Designs from India
ISBN 88-7070-050-X

REF.-BOOK 6
Copyright-free Images of Frames & Borders, Classical / Modern Style
ISBN 88-7070-051-8

REF.-BOOK # 7
New Variations of Modern Label - Designs
ISBN 88-7070-061-5

GRAFIX 1 (Theme: Fantasy)
Clip-Art Layout & Desktop
Graphic Design (Copyright-free)
ISBN 88-7070-106-9

GRAFIX 2 (Theme: Fantasy)
Clip-Art Layout & Desktop
Graphic Design (Copyright-free)
ISBN 88-7070-107-7

GRAFIX 3 (Theme: Fantasy)
Clip-Art Layout & Desktop
Graphic Design (Copyright-free)
ISBN 88-7070-108-5

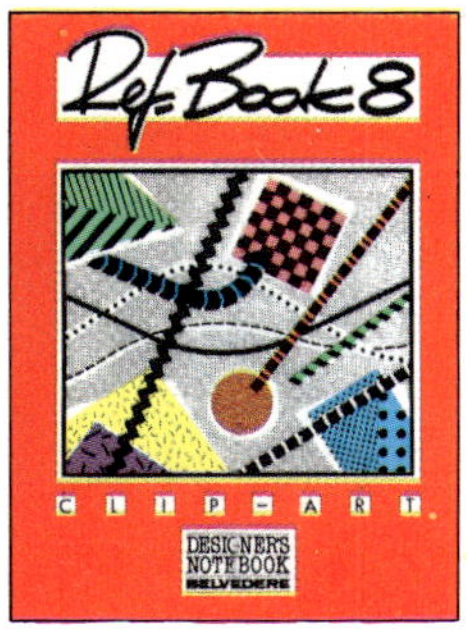

REF.-BOOK # 8
High Profession
Practical Design - Material
ISBN 88-7070-062-3

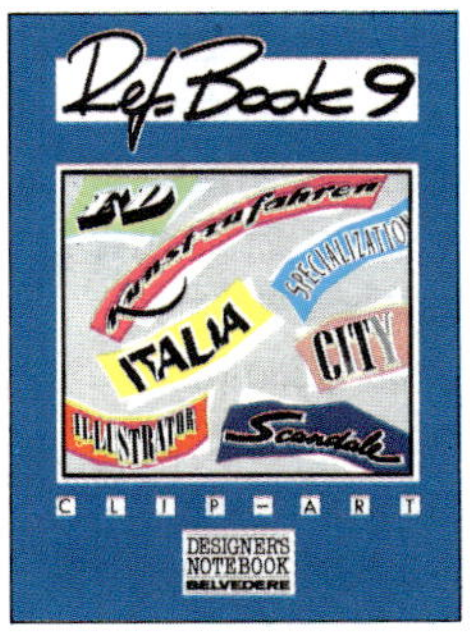

REF.-BOOK # 9
Copyright-free Variation of Letterings, Titles & Logotypes
ISBN 88-7070-151-4

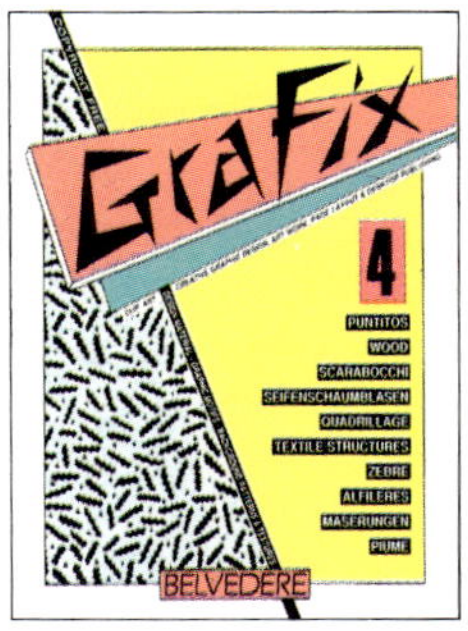

GRAFIX 4 (Theme: Harmony)
Clip-Art Layout & Desktop
Graphic Design (Copyright-free)
ISBN 88-7070-109-3

GRAFIX 5 (Theme: Harmony)
Clip-Art Layout & Desktop
Graphic Design (Copyright-free)
ISBN 88-7070-110-7

GRAFIX 6 (Theme: Harmony)
Clip-Art Layout & Desktop
Graphic Design (Copyright-free)
ISBN 88-7070-111-5

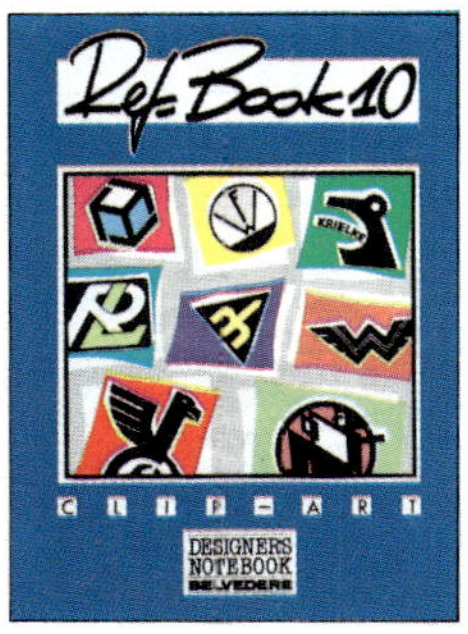

REF.-BOOK # 10
Copyright-free Graphic Selection of Symbols & Trademarks
ISBN 88-7070-152-2

REF.-BOOK # 11
Compositions & Montages & Layout & Styling
ISBN 88-7070-153-0

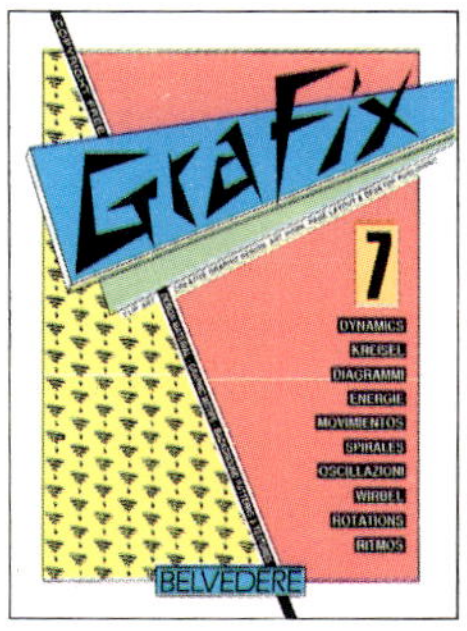

GRAFIX 7 (Theme: Geometry)
Clip-Art Layout & Desktop
Graphic Design (Copyright-free)
ISBN 88-7070-112-3

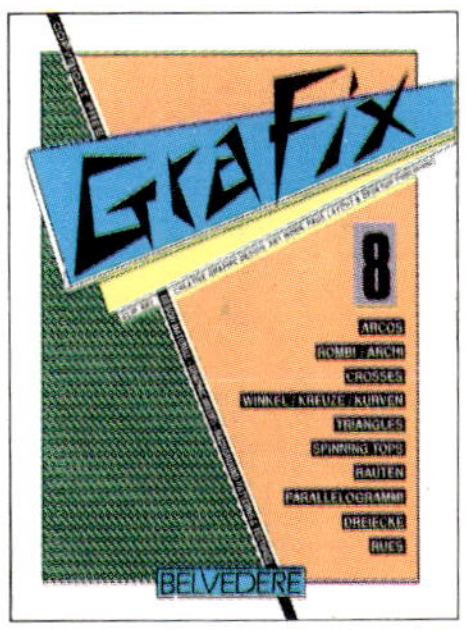

GRAFIX 8 (Theme: Geometry)
Clip-Art Layout & Desktop
Graphic Design (Copyright-free)
ISBN 88-7070-113-1

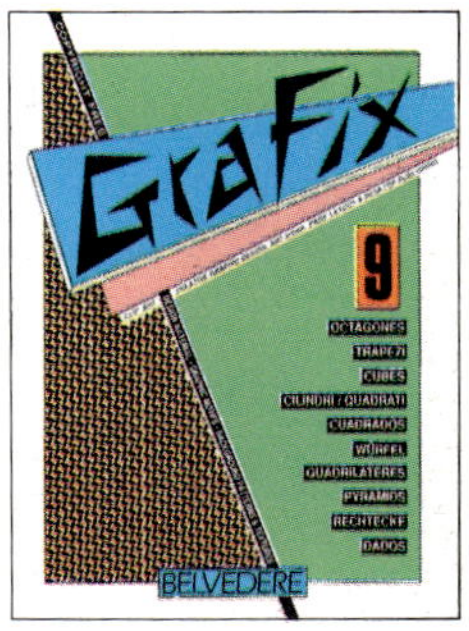

GRAFIX 9 (Theme: Geometry)
Clip-Art Layout & Desktop
Graphic Design (Copyright-free)
ISBN 88-7070-114-X